Dear Eric,

You will find enclosed just one example of the anticipated liability of Credit Card Companies who have perpetuated the financial scandal of our generation, namely; Collateralised Credit Exploitation (CCE) which is characterized as unwarranted entrapment which interminably indentures some of their best clients to long term financial slavery. This example serves to represent the 'Billions which will be repaid to Millions' due to Credit Card Companies cynically and persistently exploiting vulnerable customers from whom they are reputed to gain 50% of their corporate profits. CCE has been established as carrying NO 'Value at Risk', NO Probability of Risk with an amount at risk of NIL but most tellingly where they have already been *repaid* their capital at up to 11x the original sum they still charge unwarranted, usurious and extortionate interest rates, fees and charges on their most vulnerable customers. Treating their BEST customers as 'can be abused junk accounts' when they are proven AAA+ is clearly & demonstrably 'fraudulently counterfactual'. The 'corporately designed' failure of Credit Card Companies to make a simple and generally accepted risk weighted calculation on CCE client credit cards (up to 1,151% positive return has been estimated) have been universally condemned as being unreasonable & exploitative.

How MUCH is ENOUGH!!!

Collateralised Credit Exploitation as practised on AAA None Defaulting accounts is in effect an Annuity in Perpetuity and is demonstrably Exploitative by Design -Extortionate by Intent - Fraudulent by Nature.

Our political & regulatory & financial establishment has demonstrated endogenously heterodoxical behaviour in their collective incapacity to respect the UK Citizen by ignoring the fact of and the damage caused by Collateralised Credit Exploitation.

Exploitative By Design - Extortionate By Intent - Fraudulent By Nature
Genesis: Billions will be REPAID to Millions – Amy Lenander – Capital One
https://www.amazon.co.uk/dp/171786273X

Billions will be repaid to Millions' estimated cost to Credit Card Companies of Collateralised Credit Exploitation is conservatively put at between £50-75 Billion. Collateralised Credit Exploitation by Credit Card Companies is the cynical long term exploitation of vulnerable customers where there is no risk and no probability of risk to Credit Card Companies who perpetuate the practice.

One Example amongst millions, follows;

New Day Opus £ 110,000 gross on 10,000 @ 48.1% over 20 years*
New Day Marbles £ 84,000 gross on 9,000 @ 39.9% over 20 years*
Capital One £ 27,000 gross on 2.500 @ 31.1% over 20 years*
MBNA £ 76,000 gross on 8,000 @ 30.0% over 20 years*,
£ 46,000 gross on 5.000 @ 30.0% over 20 years*,
£ 12,000 gross on 3,000 @ 30.0% over 20 years*
BarclayCard £ 43,000 gross on 5.500 @ 26.5% over 20 years*

£ 20,000 gross on 3,000 @ 26.5% over 20 years*

RBS £ 85,000 gross on 14,000 @ 16.9% over 20 years*

£ **503**,000 to be **repaid** on £ **54,000**

*Each Credit Card to confirm exact extortion period & exploitative interest rate.

All amounts above are **PLUS** interest, charges, fees, fines & compensation conservatively creating a **£754.500** Collateralised Credit Exploitation Liability on 1) on six credit card companies (above) on 2) nine numbered cards over 20 exemplary years. Base Rate 0.25% to 0.50%. Credit Card Companies have been allowed to insidiously develop over time a purposefully distorted Credit Risk Analysis Model which effectively penalizes their best customers & imbalances the relationship between avaricious providers & vulnerable users of credit instruments. Collateralized Credit Exploitation clearly demonstrates that the 'Value at Risk' nexus does NOT exist for the Credit Card Company & that they are imposing unreasonable and extortionate charges onto the consumer. Rather than 'know' they are 'ignoring the rights & abasing the needs' of their customers.

Credit Card Companies have been allowed to insidiously develop over time a purposefully distorted Credit Risk Analysis Model which effectively penalizes their best customers and imbalances the relationship between avaricious providers & vulnerable users of credit instruments.

'Collateralized Credit Exploitation or CCE (Cynical Long Term Revolver Entrapment) is the scourge of our generation perpetrated with impunity by Credit Card Companies'

We have recently published our TimeOutCreditCards Exploitation Index (CCE Scandal Scenario) as follows: No.1 = No Counter Party Risk, No. 2 = Annuity in Perpetuity, No.3 = AAA None Defaulting, No.4 = PFI - PPI of which CCE is the greatest injustice, No.5 = Unregulated Financial Misconduct, No.6 = Unjustified Financial Exploitation, No.7 = Persistent Imperious Exploitation, No.8 = Abuse of any generally acceptable prudential regime, No 9 = Devoid of commonly accepted rationality or merit No. 10 = Fails any and every measure of financial risk based ethical behavior.

Interested parties across the world have now been invited to join the Movement @TimeOutCreditCards #PutAnEndToFinancialSlavery.

Several connected publications and keynote presentations are available T.V. Radio & Social, Business & Trade Media notified. Legacy Societal Adverse Impacts & Abusive Effects - Just ONE Example

Principal (with 9 cards from 6 companies MBNA, Capital One, RBS, BarclayCard, New Day Opus & Marbles) £ 54,000 Amount Repaid (estimated over 20 years) £ 503.000. 9 x Credit Cards from 6 Credit Card Companies interest up to 48.1% (base rate 0.25% to 0.50%). Risk Weighted Asset - up to 1,151% positive return. After almost 20 years as an impeccable payer our borrower asked politely over a period of time (2013 - 2018) 9 Credit Card companies to reduce their high rates of up to 48%+ so that they could be paid off, ALL REFUSED !!!

Repayment of those 9 cards on a principal amount of £ 54,000will have up to 20 years incur estimated gross payments of £ 503,000 (each credit card company has been asked to provide accurate payment amounts or engage in constructive discussion with the payee but each has effectively declined to do so) No financial organization has the right to impose a combination of excessive and unwarranted interest + charges + punitive fees on nominal amounts that cannot be paid back within an individual's lifetime by creating sustained (Collateralized Credit Exploitation) CCEs at rates which are not supported by any rational, reasonable, ethical measure or by any accepted financial risk ratios or prudential regime.

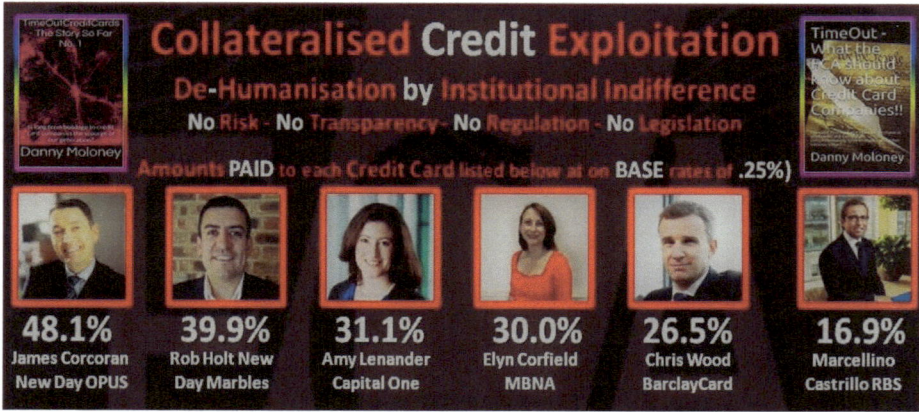

De Humanization by Institutional Indifference

Genesis: Billions will be REPAID to Millions – Amy Lenander – Capital One
https://www.amazon.co.uk/dp/171786273X

Principal - £54,000   Estimated Amount Repaid** - £503,000
Over Length of Time* - 0 to 20 years
Credit Card Interest – up to 48.1%
Bank of England Base Rate – 0.25 % to 0.50%

Amount to be repaid by the Credit Card Companies
Principal + OverPayment + Interest + Charges + Compensation =
£ 503.000*** (estimate)

Status - Creditor of each credit card named above

CCE Value at Risk (VaR) Time Frame - Lifetime, Amount at Risk - NIL, Probability of Risk - NIL, Collateralized Credit Exploitation is cynical long term entrapment & unconscionable financial slavery where there is No Risk - No Transparency - No Regulation - No Legislation.

*Each Credit Card Company have to date withheld the necessary information to make an accurate calculation of total payments made ** Each Credit Card Company can provide a more detailed breakdown. *** Projection. Account Number for 9 x cards ending (available)

How MUCH is ENOUGH!!!

Collateralised Credit Exploitation is practiced on AAA None Defaulting accounts & is in effect an Annuity in Perpetuity and is demonstrably Exploitative by Design -Extortionate by Intent - Fraudulent by Nature.

Our political & regulatory & financial establishment has demonstrated endogenously heterodoxical behaviour in their collective incapacity to respect the UK Citizen by ignoring the fact of and the damage caused by Collateralised Credit Exploitation.

Danny Moloney, MBA, MSc, MA, MAPCE, MACT (DBA IP).
Greater Eccles, Manchester, United Kingdom.
Sunday 8th July 2018

Find Out More On: https://bit.ly/2KWhfSu @TimeOutCCards @DisCreditCards *and/or*
TimeOutCreditCards: The Story So Far No. 1 https://www.amazon.co.uk/dp/B01N393PDI
What The FCA Should Know About Credit Cards https://www.amazon.co.uk/dp/B073Z1YVNT
Chronolog: Financial Slavery to Credit Cards https://www.amazon.co.uk/dp/B07FM664XV
Chronolog: 'Talk To Us, Prime Minister' https://www.amazon.co.uk/dp/B07FC2TJHY
Genesis: Billions will be REPAID to Millions – Amy Lenander – Capital One
https://www.amazon.co.uk/dp/171786273X

Breaking Free of the Shackles of Financial Slavery

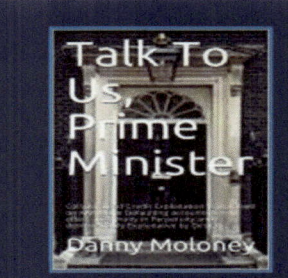

Talk to us, Prime Minister

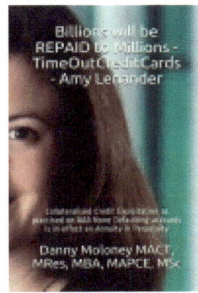

These books have already been published in both EBook & PBook Formats

Genesis: Billions will be REPAID to Millions – Amy Lenander – Capital One

https://www.amazon.co.uk/dp/171786273X

Project SafeGuard - Interminable Servitude

Collateralized Credit Exploitation is the cynical long term exploitation of vulnerable clients by Credit Card Companies, namely **Capital One**

Collateralized Credit Exploitation is Exploitative by Design – Extortionate by Intent - Fraudulent by Nature. Exemplified as where there is **NO** financial or Value at risk and the principal has been repaid 11x times to **Capital One** (incl predecessors). **Estimated** Gross Amount ALREADY Paid over 20 years stands at **£27,000** (estimated subject to data being provided by you)

Specifically with regards to the behaviour of **Capital One** please respond to the following;

Why are you charging **35+%** when the Bank of England base rate is 0.25 % to 0.50%?
Why do you take such advantage of an account which has been paying you for nearly 20 years?
Why is there **NO** Transparency in your dealings with our account?
Why have you failed to respond to our letters from 2013 - 2014 - 2015 - 2016 - 2017 - 2018?
Why have you failed in your Procedures – Polices – Processes to protect your client?
Why do you display so much Institutional Indifference to the well being of our account?
Why as we have paid **Capital One** so much already, should pay you any more money?

Collateralised Credit Exploitation by Credit Card Companies has meant up to 20 years of paying extortionate interest rates, fees and charges providing each of NINE cards from SIX companies with a guaranteed return of over 1140%, with NO risk on their part. It has meant no holidays, no social life, not being able to pay for my daughter's wedding, not being able to buy my children and or grandchildren any birthday or Christmas presents, no house repairs, no clothes, no car (previous one sold to pay for credit card bills 12 years ago). Having to take out a mortgage (on an unmortgaged property to pay for credit card bills 12 years ago). Serious health affects, always having to walk (rain or shine) and having to shop in pound stores. All the money repaid amounting to a conservative £ **503,000** on a principal of only £54,000 has been fuelling the insatiable beast, to whom the account is one of their most profitable customers!!

How MUCH is ENOUGH!!!

Collateralised Credit Exploitation as practiced on AAA None Defaulting accounts is in effect an Annuity in Perpetuity and is demonstrably Exploitative by Design -Extortionate by Intent - Fraudulent by Nature. Andrew Bailey from the FCA has dealt with the immediate outstanding balance with what he terms Persistent Debt* (this £54,000 will be repaid by each credit card companies in September) but he has yet to deal with Persistent Exploitation which is the Collateralised Credit Exploitation i.e. the £27,000.

The Credit Card Companies know that they will always get paid whatever the 'cost' to the lives of their customers. Collateralised Credit Exploitation is financial slavery and has led to interminable servitude. *Note: Persistent Debt regulations by the FCA specify that **Capital One** will discharge the principal amount (circa £2,500) on this account at their own cost which leaves an estimated balance of £24,000 payable to the account holder.

BBA Letter One 27th June 2017 – Anthony Browne
Greater Eccles, Manchester, M30 7AZ
Telephone: 0161 789 8787   Email: timeoutcreditcards@globalmehpte.com

Anthony Browne
Chief Executive Officer
British Bankers Association
Pinners Hall
105 - 108 Old Broad Street
London, EC2N 1EX   Tuesday 27th June 2017

Are **Policy Makers** (Government) & **Prudential Oversighters** (Regulators) aware of the true and full extent of Collateralised Credit Exploitation (CCE) of Good Customers by Credit Card Companies? is this (described by some) as the corporate misbehavior / malpractice financial scandal of the century?? greater than CDOs and PPIs **COMBINED???**

Dear Mr Browne,   Credit Cards: **1997 - 2007 - 2017 - 2027**

We note the recent initiative of the Financial Conduct Authority (FCA) with respect to their study of the charges / fees / interest made (unjustly & incorrectly, we believe) by Credit Cards Companies pursuant to their 'regularized' behaviors & practices in particular to the 'management' of long term client PBS rated accounts, people whom we term & refer to, as their 'Good Customers'. We have today forwarded our initial submission directly to the Financial Conduct Authority within the specified deadline date of 3rd July 2017. This submission is of significant interest and import to the Board of the British Bankers Association, your members & especially to the General Public, Media and the wider financial industry and community.

In order to represent our submission to the widest possible audience within the regulatory financial sector, we have also sent a short synopsis of our submission to;

1) **The British Bankers Association**, 2) The Finance & Leasing Association, 3) The Financial Conduct Authority, 4) The Financial Ombudsman, 5) The UK Parliament (to prepare for future legislation), 6) The Lending & Standards Board, 7) The Prudential Regulation Authority, 8) The UK Cards Association, 9) The Competition & Markets Authority, 10) The Payment Systems Regulator, 11) The Money Advice Service and 12) TBC.

In addition and in support of our submission, we have and will be publishing the following;

TimeOutCreditCards 1 - The Story So Far - **Credit Card Companies**
(Published 27th January 2017) Available Now. Audience Reach to Date - 10,000s

TimeOutCreditCards 2 - The Story So Far - **The Regulators**
(To be Published 3 July 2017) Audience Reach Anticipated - 100,000s

TimeOutCreditCards 3 - The Story So Far - **The Investigation**
(To Be Published on FCA Report) Audience Reach Anticipated - 000,000,000s

TimeOutCreditCards 4 - The Story so Far - **The Legislation**
(To Be Published on FCA Aftermath) Audience Reach Anticipated - +000,000,000s

Yours Sincerely,

Danny Moloney, MBA,

Manchester, UK

BBA Letter Two 15th April 2018 – Eric Leenders

Greater Eccles, Manchester, M30 7AZ

Telephone: 0161 789 8787   Email: timeoutcreditcards@globalmehpte.com

Eric Leenders
Chief Executive Officer
British Bankers Association
Pinners Hall
105 - 108 Old Broad Street
London, EC2N 1EX   Sunday 15th April 2018

Dear Eric,

Following our earlier letter to the British Bankers Association of 27th June 2017 last.

We write to you now concerning Collateralized Credit Exploitation or with direct reference to the Financial Conduct Authority's recently published study on 'Persistent Debt' what is now being referred to as 'Persistent Exploitation' by Credit Card Companies.

We attach overleaf a courtesy copy of a letter sent to Mrs. Theresa May in the hope that she may be able to help to bring such Unregulated Credit Card Company Behavior to a swift equitable denouement and that you may make a contribution to that long overdue debate on behalf of the British Bankers Association.

Yours Sincerely,

Danny Moloney, MBA.

Letter One 15th April 2018 - Theresa May

Greater Eccles, Manchester, M30 7AZ

Telephone: 0161 789 8787   Email: timeoutcreditcards@globalmehpte.com

Mrs. Theresa May,
10 Downing Street,
Westminster
London,
SW 1A 2AA

Theresa May - 1

April 15th 2018

'The financialisation of our economy has rendered political institutions virtually powerless to represent the interests of UK consumers'.

Dear Mrs. May,

I write on this occasion to represent millions of U.K. citizens, who daily labor under the insidious burden of Collateralised Credit Exploitation (a perversely distorted and financially reprehensible loan to payment ratio) perpetrated by the named Credit Card Companies and tacitly supported by the Government Bodies, Authorities & Associations, also named below.

Andrew Bailey at the FCA has attempted to deal with the scandal by addressing 'Persistent Debt' but the real issue is 'Persistent Exploitation' by unregulated Credit Card Companies.

Credit Card Companies - The Perpetrators

MBNA - Elyn Corfield ,   OPUS - James Corcoran,   MARBLES - Rob Holt,   Royal Bank of Scotland - Marcellino Castrillo,   Capital One - Amy Lenander,   Barclaycard - Chris Wood

Government Bodies & Authorities & Associations - The Regulators

Financial Ombudsman - Caroline Wayman, Prudential Regulation Authority - Mark Carney, Competition & Markets Authority - Andrea Coscelli, Payment Systems Regulator - Hannah Nixon, Philip Hammond - Chancellor of the Exchequer, Andrew Bailey - Financial Conduct Authority, UK Cards Association - Graham Peacop, Finance & Leasing Association - Richard Jones, British Bankers Association - Eric Leenders, Lending & Standards - Board Dave Pickering & Money Advice Service - Charles Counsell.

I would like you to invite those named above to meet with you and I at 10 Downing Street, the seat of our executive government to answer the questions from myself, 1) Why the Credit Card Companies & the Government Bodies & Authorities have behaved like this and effectively allowed this scandal to persist & from you; 2) What are they going to do about it?

Thanks for your support in resolving this demonstrable and injurious evil within our society.
Danny Moloney
Greater Eccles, Manchester, United Kingdom

BBA Letter Three 14th May – Eric Leenders
Greater Eccles, Manchester, M30 7AZ

Telephone: 0161 789 8787   Email: timeoutcreditcards@globalmehpte.com

Eric Leenders
Chief Executive Officer
British Bankers Association
Pinners Hall
105 - 108 Old Broad Street
London, EC2N 1EX   Monday 14th May 2018

'**Collateralized Credit Exploitation or CCE** (Cynical Long Term Revolver Entrapment)
is the scourge of our generation perpetrated with impunity by Credit Card Companies'

Dear Eric,

Further to our letter to you of Sunday 15/4/18, to which we await your reply.

We have recently published our **TimeOutCreditCards Exploitation Index** (CCE Scandal Scenario) as follows: **No.**1 = No Counter Party Risk, **No.** 2 = Annuity in Perpetuity, **No.**3 = AAA None Defaulting, **No.**4 = PFI - PPI of which CCE is the greatest injustice, **No.5** = Unregulated Financial Misconduct, **No.**6 = Unjustified Financial Exploitation, **No.7** = Persistent Impunious Exploitation, **No.8** = Abuse of any generally acceptable prudential regime, **No 9** = Devoid of commonly accepted rationality or merit **No. 10** = Fails any and every measure of financial risk based ethical behavior.

Interested parties across the world have now been invited to join the Movement @TimeOutCreditCards #PutAnEndToFinancialSlavery. Several connected publications and keynote presentations are available T.V. Radio & Social, Business & Trade Media notified.

Thank you for your support in resolving this demonstrable, injurious, flagrant and persistent financial slavery within our society.

Danny Moloney, Restitutional Activist, Greater Eccles, Manchester, United Kingdom

Legacy Societal Adverse Impacts & Abusive Effects - Just ONE Example

Principal (with 9 cards from 6 companies MBNA, Capital One, RBS, BarclayCard, New Day Opus & Marbles) **£ 60.799** Amount Repaid (estimated over 20 years) **£ 472.001** Amount which will be Repaid (estimated over 30 years) **£ 699.933.** 9 x Credit Cards from 6 Credit Card Companies interest up to 48.1% (base rate 0.25% to 0.50%). Risk Weighted Asset - up to **1,151%** positive return. After almost 20 years as an impeccable payer our borrower asked politely over a period of time (2013 - 2017) 9 Credit Card companies to reduce their high rates of up to 48%+ so that they could be paid off, **ALL REFUSED !!!**

Repayment of those 9 cards on a principal amount of £ 60,799 will have up to 20 years incur estimated gross payments of £ 472,001 and over 30 years will incur estimated gross payments of £ 699,933 (each credit card company has been asked to provide accurate payment amounts or engage in constructive discussion with the payee but each has effectively declined to do so) No financial organization has the right to impose a combination of excessive and unwarranted interest + charges + punitive fees on nominal amounts that cannot be paid back within an individual's lifetime by creating sustained (Collateralized Credit Exploitation)

CCEs at rates which are not supported by any rational, reasonable, ethical measure or by any accepted financial risk ratios or prudential regime.

Principal - **£60,799**   Estimated Amount Repaid** - **£472,001**
Over Length of Time* - **0** to **20 years**
Credit Card Interest – up to **48.1%**
Bank of England Base Rate – 0.25 % to **0.50%**

Amount to be repaid by the Credit Card Companies
Principal + OverPayment + Interest + Charges + Compensation = £ 350,403.00***
(estimate)

Status - Creditor of each credit card named above.
*Each Credit Card Company have to date withheld the necessary information to make an accurate calculation of total payments made ** Each Credit Card Company can provide a more detailed breakdown. *** Projection. Account for 9 x cards ending (available)

BBA Letter Four 20th June – Eric Leenders
Greater Eccles, Manchester, M30 7AZ
Telephone: 0161 789 8787   Email: timeoutcreditcards@globalmehpte.com

Eric Leenders   Eric Leenders - 4
Chief Executive Officer
British Bankers Association
Pinners Hall
105 - 108 Old Broad Street
London, EC2N 1EX   Wednesday 20th June 2018

Dear Eric, **Billions will be repaid to Millions of UK Consumers**

Further to our letters to you of 15/4/18 & 14/5/18, to which we await your reply.

We look forward to the Collateralized Credit Exploitation Summit to be held at Downing Street, which will be followed by presentations across the country entitled 'Ending Financial Slavery to Credit Card Companies'.

Thank you for your support in resolving this demonstrable, injurious, flagrant and persistent financial evil within our society.

Danny Moloney
Restitutional Activist
Greater Eccles, Manchester, United Kingdom

Legacy Societal Adverse Impacts & Abusive Effects - Just ONE Example
We have recently published our **TimeOutCreditCards Exploitation Index** (CCE Scandal Scenario) as follows: **No.1** = No Counter Party Risk, **No. 2** = Annuity in Perpetuity, **No.3** = AAA None Defaulting, **No.4** = PFI - PPI of which CCE is the greatest injustice, **No.5** = Unregulated Financial Misconduct, **No.6** = Unjustified Financial Exploitation, **No.7** = Persistent Impunious Exploitation, **No.8** = Abuse of any generally acceptable prudential regime, **No 9** = Devoid of commonly accepted rationality or merit **No. 10** = Fails any and every measure of financial risk based ethical behavior.

Principal (with 9 cards from 6 companies MBNA, Capital One, RBS, BarclayCard, New Day Opus & Marbles)) **£ 60.799** Amount Repaid (estimated over 20 years) **£ 472.001** Amount which will be Repaid (estimated over 30 years) **£ 699.933.** 9 x Credit Cards from 6 Credit Card Companies interest up to 48.1% (base rate 0.25% to 0.50%) Risk Weighted Asset - up to **1,151%** positive return. After almost 20 years as an impeccable payer our borrower asked politely over a period of time (2013 - 2017) 9 Credit Card companies to reduce their high rates of up to 48%+ so that they could be paid off, **ALL REFUSED !!!**

Repayment of those 9 cards on a principal amount of £ 60,799 will have up to 20 years incur estimated gross payments of £ 472,001 and over 30 years will incur estimated gross payments of £ 699,933 (each credit card company has been asked to provide accurate payment amounts or engage in constructive discussion with the payee but each has effectively declined to do so) No financial organization has the right to impose a combination of excessive and unwarranted interest + charges + punitive fees on nominal amounts that cannot be paid back within an individual's lifetime by creating sustained (Collateralized Credit Exploitation) CCEs at rates which are not supported by any rational, reasonable, ethical measure or by any accepted financial risk ratios or prudential regime.

Principal - **£60,799**

Estimated Amount Repaid** - **£472,001**

Over Length of Time* - **0 to 20 years**

Credit Card Interest – up to **48.1%**

Bank of England Base Rate – 0.25 % to **0.50%**

Amount to be repaid by the Credit Card Companies
Principal + OverPayment + Interest + Charges + Compensation = £ 350,403.00***

(estimate)

Status - Creditor of each credit card named above.

*Each Credit Card Company have to date withheld the necessary information to make an accurate calculation of total payments made ** Each Credit Card Company can provide a more detailed breakdown. *** Projection. Account for 9 x cards ending (available)

BBA Letter Five 9th July – Eric Leenders

Greater Eccles, Manchester, M30 7AZ

Telephone: 0161 789 8787   Email: timeoutcreditcards@globalmehpte.com

Eric Leenders Eric Leenders - 5
Chief Executive Officer
British Bankers Association
Pinners Hall
105 - 108 Old Broad Street
London, EC2N 1EX   Monday 9th July 2018

Dear Eric,

You will find overleaf just one example of the anticipated liability of Credit Card Companies who have perpetuated the financial scandal of our generation, namely; Collateralized Credit Exploitation (CCE) which is characterized as unwarranted entrapment which interminably indentures some of their best clients to long term financial slavery. This example serves to represent the 'Billions which will be repaid to Millions' due to Credit Card Companies cynically and persistently exploiting vulnerable customers from whom they are reputed to gain 50% of their corporate profits. CCE has been established as carrying **NO** 'Value at Risk', **NO** 'Probability of Risk' with an amount at risk of **NIL** but most tellingly where they have already been *repaid* their capital at up to **11x** the original sum they still charge unwarranted, usurious and extortionate interest rates, fees and charges on their most vulnerable customers. Treating their BEST customers as 'can be abused junk accounts' when they are proven AAA+ is clearly & demonstrably 'fraudulently counterfactual'. The 'corporately designed' failure of Credit Card Companies to make a simple and generally accepted risk weighted calculation on CCE client credit cards (up to 1,151% positive return has been estimated) have been universally condemned as being unreasonable & exploitative.

How MUCH is ENOUGH!!!

Collateralised Credit Exploitation is practiced on AAA None Defaulting accounts & is in effect an Annuity in Perpetuity and is demonstrably Exploitative by Design -Extortionate by Intent - Fraudulent by Nature.

Our political & regulatory & financial establishment has demonstrated endogenously heterodoxical behaviour in their collective incapacity to respect the UK Citizen by ignoring the fact of and the damage caused by Collateralised Credit Exploitation.

Danny Moloney,
MBA, MSc, MA, MAPCE, MACT (DBA IP).
Greater Eccles, Manchester, United Kingdom.
Sunday 8th July 2018

Exploitative By Design - Extortionate By Intent - Fraudulent By Nature

Billions will be repaid to Millions' estimated cost to Credit Card Companies of Collateralised Credit Exploitation is conservatively put at between £50-75 Billion. Collateralised Credit Exploitation by Credit Card Companies is the cynical long term exploitation of vulnerable customers where there is no risk and no probability of risk to Credit Card Companies who perpetuate the practice.

One Example amongst millions, follows;

*Each Credit Card to confirm exact extortion period & exploitative interest rate.
New Day Opus £ 110,000 gross on 10,000 @ 48.1% over 20 years*
New Day Marbles £ 84,000 gross on 9,000 @ 39.9% over 20 years*
Capital One £ 27,000 gross on 2.500 @ 31.1% over 20 years*
MBNA £ 76,000 gross on 8,000 @ 30.0% over 20 years*,
£ 46,000 gross on 5.000 @ 30.0% over 20 years*,
£ 12,000 gross on 3,000 @ 30.0% over 20 years*
BarclayCard £ 43,000 gross on 5.500 @ 26.5% over 20 years*
£ 20,000 gross on 3,000 @ 26.5% over 20 years*
RBS £ 85,000 gross on 14,000 @ 16.9% over 20 years*

£ 503,000 to be repaid on £ 54,000

All amounts above are **PLUS** interest, charges, fees, fines & compensation conservatively creating a £**754.500** Collateralized Credit Exploitation Liability on 1) on six credit card companies (above) on 2) nine numbered cards over 20 exemplary years. Base Rate 0.25% to 0.50%. Credit Card Companies have been allowed to insidiously develop over time a purposefully distorted Credit Risk Analysis Model which effectively penalizes their best customers & imbalances the relationship between avaricious providers & vulnerable users of credit instruments. Collateralized Credit Exploitation clearly demonstrates that the 'Value at Risk' nexus does NOT exist for the Credit Card Company & that they are imposing unreasonable and extortionate charges onto the consumer. Rather than 'know' they are 'ignoring the rights & abasing the needs' of their customers. Credit Card Companies have been allowed to insidiously develop over time a purposefully distorted Credit Risk Analysis Model which effectively penalizes their best customers and imbalances the relationship between avaricious providers & vulnerable users of credit instruments.

Find Out More On: https://bit.ly/2KWhfSu @TimeOutCCards @DisCreditCards *and/or*
TimeOutCreditCards: The Story So Far No. 1 https://www.amazon.co.uk/dp/B01N393PDI
What The FCA Should Know About Credit Cards https://www.amazon.co.uk/dp/B073Z1YVNT
Chronolog : Financial Slavery to Credit Cards https://www.amazon.co.uk/dp/B07FM664XV
Chronolog: 'Talk To Us, Prime Minister' https://www.amazon.co.uk/dp/B07FC2TJHY
Genesis: Billions will be REPAID to Millions – Amy Lenander – Capital One
https://www.amazon.co.uk/dp/171786273X

Dear Eric

You will find enclosed just one example of the anticipated liability of Credit Card Companies who have perpetuated the financial scandal of our generation, namely; Collateralized Credit Exploitation (CCE) which is characterized as unwarranted entrapment which interminably indentures some of their best clients to long term financial slavery. This example serves to represent the 'Billions which will be repaid to Millions' due to Credit Card Companies cynically and persistently exploiting vulnerable customers from whom they are reputed to gain 50% of their corporate profits. CCE has been established as carrying **NO** 'Value at Risk', **NO** 'Probability of Risk' with an amount at risk of **NIL** but most tellingly where they have already been *repaid* their capital at up to **11x** the original sum they still charge unwarranted, usurious and extortionate interest rates, fees and charges on their most vulnerable customers. Treating their BEST customers as 'can be abused junk accounts' when they are proven AAA+ is clearly & demonstrably 'fraudulently counterfactual'. The 'corporately designed' failure of Credit Card Companies to make a simple and generally accepted risk weighted calculation on CCE client credit cards (up to 1,151% positive return has been estimated) have been universally condemned as being unreasonable & exploitative.

How MUCH is ENOUGH!!!

Collateralised Credit Exploitation is practiced on AAA None Defaulting accounts & is in effect an Annuity in Perpetuity and is demonstrably Exploitative by Design -Extortionate by Intent - Fraudulent by Nature.
Our political & regulatory & financial establishment has demonstrated endogenously heterodoxical behaviour in their collective incapacity to respect the UK Citizen by ignoring the fact of and the damage caused by Collateralised Credit Exploitation.

Danny Moloney,
MBA, MSc, MA, MAPCE, MACT (DBA IP).
Greater Eccles, Manchester, United Kingdom.
Sunday 8th July 2018

Exploitative By Design - Extortionate By Intent - Fraudulent By Nature

Billions will be repaid to Millions' estimated cost to Credit Card Companies of Collateralised Credit Exploitation is conservatively put at between £50-75 Billion. Collateralised Credit Exploitation by Credit Card Companies is the cynical long term exploitation of vulnerable customers where there is no risk and no probability of risk to Credit Card Companies who perpetuate the practice.

One Example amongst millions, follows;

*Each Credit Card to confirm exact extortion period & exploitative interest rate.

New Day Opus £ 110,000 gross on 10,000 @ 48.1% over 20 years*
New Day Marbles £ 84,000 gross on 9,000 @ 39.9% over 20 years*
Capital One £ 27,000 gross on 2.500 @ 31.1% over 20 years*
MBNA £ 76,000 gross on 8,000 @ 30.0% over 20 years*,
£ 46,000 gross on 5.000 @ 30.0% over 20 years*,
£ 12,000 gross on 3,000 @ 30.0% over 20 years*
BarclayCard £ 43,000 gross on 5.500 @ 26.5% over 20 years*
£ 20,000 gross on 3,000 @ 26.5% over 20 years*

RBS £ 85,000 gross on 14,000 @ 16.9% over 20 years*

£ 503,000 to be repaid on **£ 54,000**

All amounts above are **PLUS** interest, charges, fees, fines & compensation conservatively creating a **£754.500** Collateralized Credit Exploitation Liability on 1) on six credit card companies (above) on 2) nine numbered cards over 20 exemplary years. Base Rate 0.25% to 0.50%. Credit Card Companies have been allowed to insidiously develop over time a purposefully distorted Credit Risk Analysis Model which effectively penalizes their best customers & imbalances the relationship between avaricious providers & vulnerable users of credit instruments. Collateralized Credit Exploitation clearly demonstrates that the 'Value at Risk' nexus does NOT exist for the Credit Card Company & that they are imposing unreasonable and extortionate charges onto the consumer. Rather than 'know' they are 'ignoring the rights & abasing the needs' of their customers. Credit Card Companies have been allowed to insidiously develop over time a purposefully distorted Credit Risk Analysis Model which effectively penalizes their best customers and imbalances the relationship between avaricious providers & vulnerable users of credit instruments.

Find Out More On: https://bit.ly/2KWhfSu @TimeOutCCards @DisCreditCards *and/or*
TimeOutCreditCards: The Story So Far No. 1 https://www.amazon.co.uk/dp/B01N393PDI
What The FCA Should Know About Credit Cards https://www.amazon.co.uk/dp/B073Z1YVNT
Chronolog : Financial Slavery to Credit Cards https://www.amazon.co.uk/dp/B07FM664XV
Chronolog: 'Talk To Us, Prime Minister' https://www.amazon.co.uk/dp/B07FC2TJHY
Genesis: Billions will be REPAID to Millions – Amy Lenander – Capital One
https://www.amazon.co.uk/dp/171786273X

TimeOutCreditCards

Collateralised Credit Exploitation

New Day Opus - New Day Marbles - Capital One - MBNA - Barclaycard - RBS

Your MOST profitable customers have rights too for Justice and Respect.

It is no surprise that James Corcoran of New Day Opus, Rob Holt of New Day Marbles, Amy Lenander of Capital One, Elyn Corfield of MBNA, Chris Wood of BarclayCard & Marcellino Castrillo of Royal Bank of Scotland, have not responded to letters sent to each one of them personally and provided a personalized response by way of explanation as to their collective behavior in perpetrating the financial scandal of our generation - Collateralized Credit Exploitation.

TimeOutCreditCards Collateralised Credit Exploitation has impaired the inherent right of individual or collective customers for equitable financial management.

If Politicians - Regulators - Credit Card Companies fail to support the best interests of a member of the public; they are entitled to take the measures necessary to maintain respect and bring an end to exploitation exemplified by TimeOutCreditCards Collateralised Credit Exploitation, which has been proven to be Credit Exploitation & Financial Slavery.

Customers are equally entitled to a level of support which should be designed and is subsequently conducted in accordance with recognized best practice and ethical standards.

Customers have the right to expect Politicians - Regulators to use commonly accepted standards commonly assess, confirm and improve their governance and financial management policies and practice and be accountable to their customers for their malpractice.

Politicians - Regulators have implicit responsibility to protect and safeguard customers from extortion by unregulated Credit Card Companies.

Collateralised Credit Exploitation is a clear case of financial exploitation, it was the very scenario that the Legislatory & Regulatory framework has been designed to confront, challenge, manage & control in the interests of consumers.

'No financial organization has the right to make excessive interest & charges on nominal amounts that cannot be paid back within an individual's lifetime by creating (Collateralised Credit Exploitation) CCEs'

""""It should be easier for consumers to challenge unfair agreements and that the definition of 'extortionate' should be widened to cover unfair practices both at the time of entering the credit agreement as well as any subsequent events that may have led to unfairness"""".

Detailed information has been provided to the 6 x Credit Card Companies
(NINE cards in total)

(MBNA Elyn Corfield - Capital One Amy Lenander - New Day Marbles Rob Holt - BarclayCard Chris Wood - RBS Marcellino Castrillo - New Day Opus - James Corcoran) who are known and are evidenced to practice Collateralised Credit Exploitation (CCE)

The Financial Conduct Authority Andrew Bailey - The Financial Ombudsman Caroline Wayman - The UK Cards Association Graham Peacop - The Prudential Regulation Authority Mark Carney - The Finance & Leasing Association Richard Jones - The British Bankers Association Eric Leenders - The Competition & Markets Authority Andrea Coscelli - The UK Parliament Phillip Hammond - The Lending & Standards Board Dave Pickering - The Payment Systems Regulator Hannah Nixon - The Money Advice Service Charles Counsell have been made fully aware of the practice of Collateralised Credit Exploitation (CCE).

EVERY Member of Parliament has victims of Collateralised Credit Exploitation in his or her constituency; suffering under the pain of unreasonable, unwarranted and unjustified behavior by Credit Card Companies.

British consumers have been slavishly providing extortionate, unjustified & unwarranted profits for Credit Card Companies for generations under the indefensibly false guise of 'long revolver credit' and are now holding them to account for their unwarranted financial profligacy of people's lives, their relationships, their income, their marriages & their life chances. Collateralised Credit Exploitation is entrapment & financial slavery

'Billions will be repaid to Millions' initial estimate of the cost to Credit Card Companies of Collateralised Credit Exploitation is conservatively put at between £50 - 75 Billion.

Exploitative By Design - Extortionate By Intent - Fraudulent By Nature

Never in the annals of financial history has so much been taken from so many by so few.

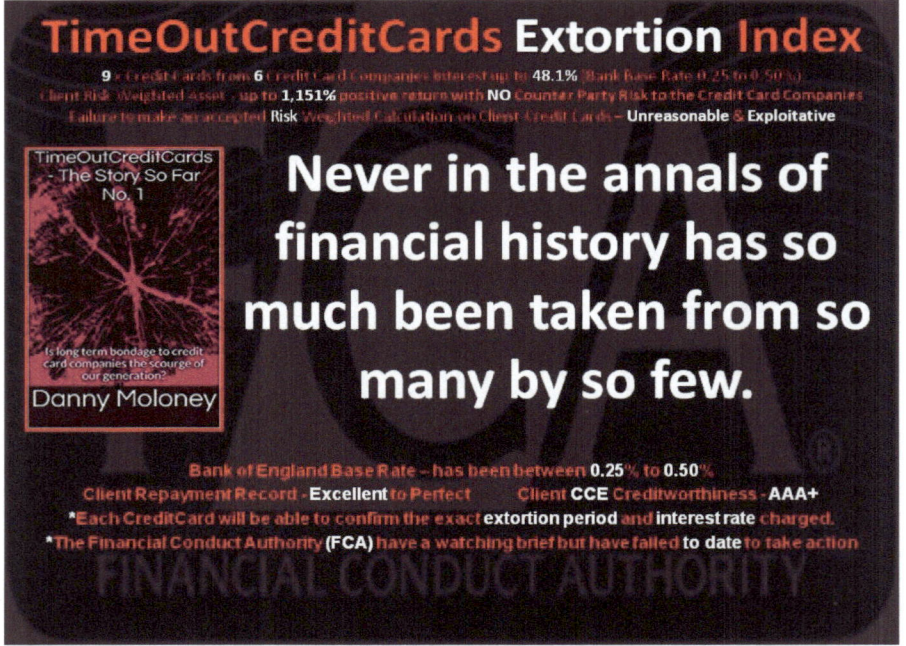

TimeOutCreditCards Collateralised Credit Exploitation: Never in the Annals of Financial History

TimeOutCreditCards Collateralised Credit Exploitation: Treating AAA+ Customers as Junk Accounts

TimeOutCreditCards Collateralised Credit Exploitation: REDlined Ending Financial Slavery

TimeOutCreditCards Collateralised Credit Exploitation: NO Risk BUT exploitative Rewards!!!

TimeOutCreditCards Collateralised Credit Exploitation: Cynical Use of Long Term Entrapment

TimeOutCreditCards Collateralised Credit Exploitation: How can Legislators & Regulators allow this to happen?

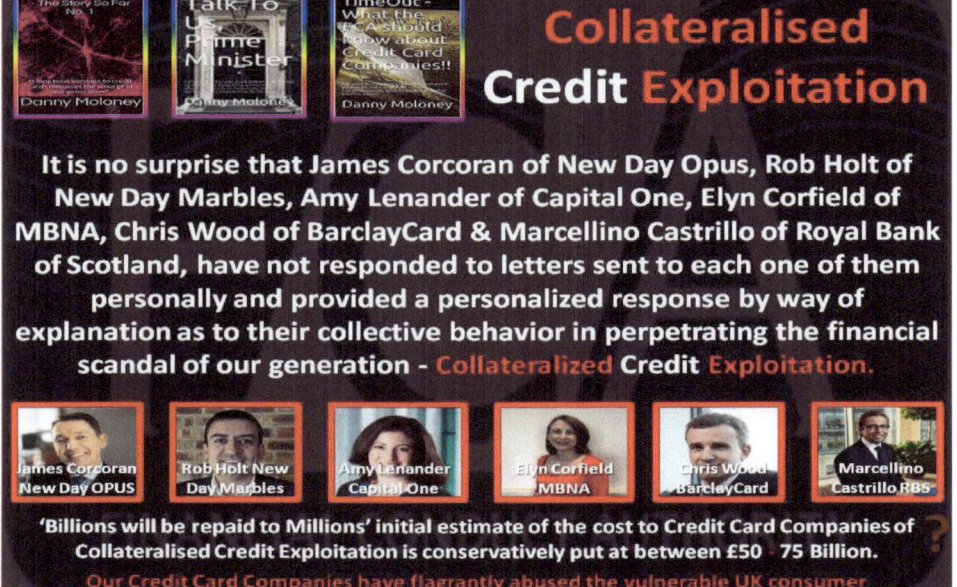

TimeOutCreditCards Collateralised Credit Exploitation: It is NO surprise that there is NO response

TimeOutCreditCards Collateralised Credit Exploitation: Billions will be REPAID to millions

TimeOutCreditCards Collateralised Credit Exploitation: Talk to us, Prime Minister

TimeOutCreditCards Collateralised Credit Exploitation: Endogenously Heterodoxical

TimeOutCreditCards Collateralised Credit Exploitation: Should PAY, Won't PAY!!!

TimeOutCreditCards Collateralised Credit Exploitation: he Who Accepts Evil

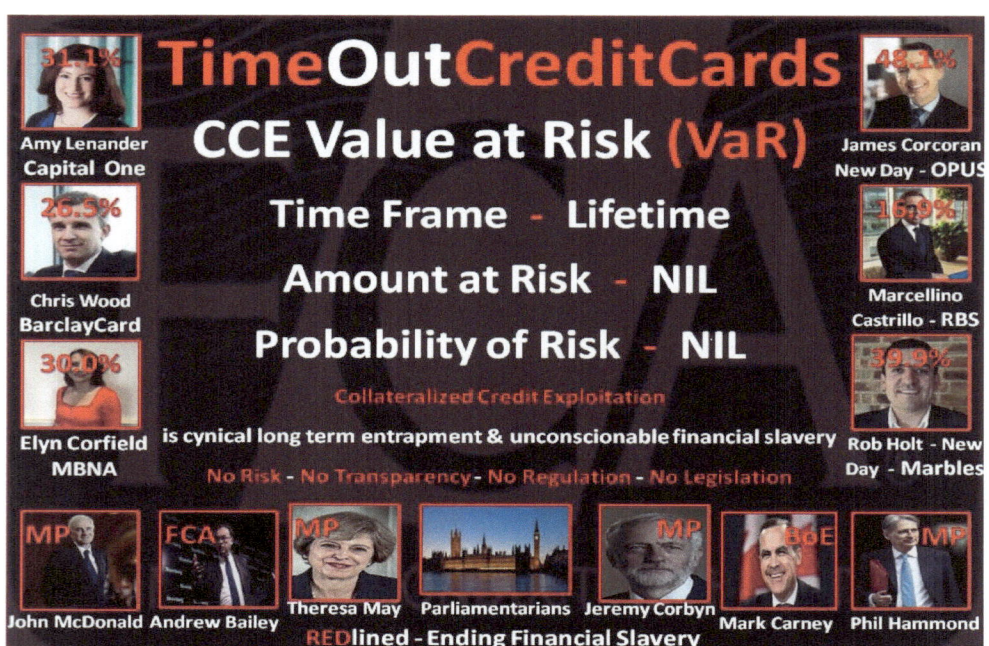

TimeOutCreditCards Collateralised Credit Exploitation: CCE Value AT Risk ?

TimeOutCreditCards Collateralised Credit Exploitation: Extortion Index

TimeOutCreditCards Collateralised Credit Exploitation: PutAnEndToFinancialSlavery

TimeOutCreditCards Collateralised Credit Exploitation: Could or Should

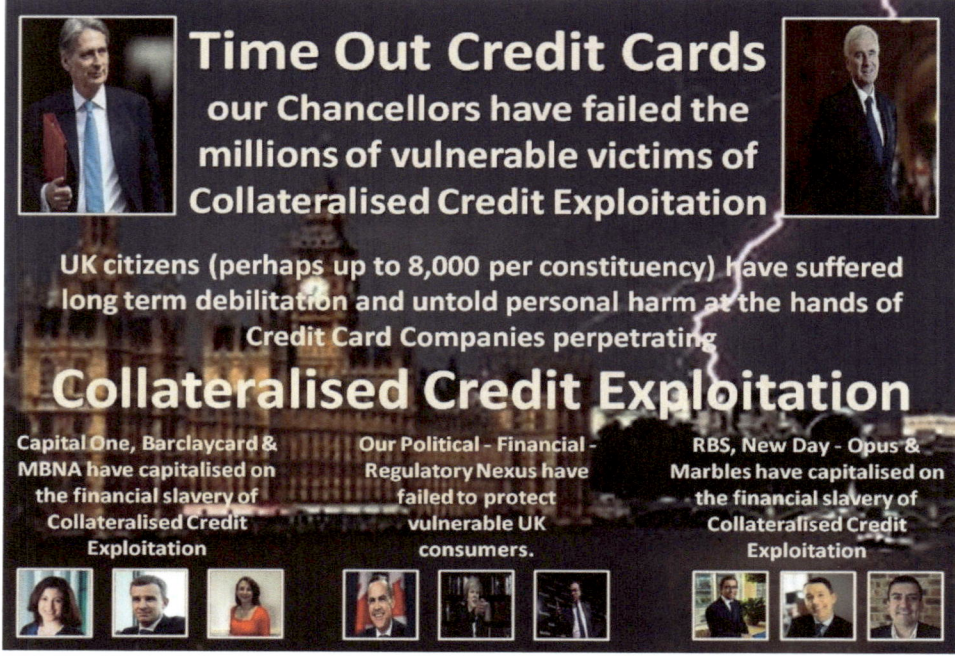

TimeOutCreditCards Collateralised Credit Exploitation: Our Chancellors have FAILED!!!

TimeOutCreditCards Collateralised Credit Exploitation: Annuity in Perpetuity

'Collateralized Credit Exploitation or CCE
(Cynical Long Term Revolver Entrapment) is the scourge of our generation perpetrated with impunity by Credit Card Companies'

  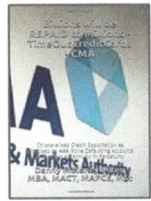

Collateralised Credit Exploitation as practised on AAA None Defaulting Accounts is in effect an Annuity in Perpetuity and is demonstrably
Exploitative by Design - Extortionate by Intent - Fraudulent by Nature.

TimeOutCreditCards Collateralised Credit Exploitation: Perpetrators

Andrew Bailey

https://www.amazon.co.uk/dp/B07FS458HK

https://www.amazon.co.uk/dp/1717858147

Theresa May

https://www.amazon.co.uk/dp/B07FS2CPWG

https://www.amazon.co.uk/dp/1717857310

James Corcoran

https://www.amazon.co.uk/dp/B07FS3QPQC

https://www.amazon.co.uk/dp/1717862241

Rob Holt

https://www.amazon.co.uk/dp/B07FS7G7QS

https://www.amazon.co.uk/dp/1717862411

Amy Lenander

https://www.amazon.co.uk/dp/B07FS3GYBW

https://www.amazon.co.uk/dp/171786273X

Elyn Corfield

https://www.amazon.co.uk/dp/B07FS4WS71

https://www.amazon.co.uk/dp/1717863027

Chris Wood

https://www.amazon.co.uk/dp/B07FS5FPQ7

https://www.amazon.co.uk/dp/1717863671

Marcellino Castrillo

https://www.amazon.co.uk/dp/B07FS9317M

https://www.amazon.co.uk/dp/1717863930

Mark Carney

https://www.amazon.co.uk/dp/B07FSBWZ3C

https://www.amazon.co.uk/dp/1717864961

Andrea Costelli

https://www.amazon.co.uk/dp/B07FSFSGPY

https://www.amazon.co.uk/dp/1717865402

Jeremy Corbyn

https://www.amazon.co.uk/dp/B07FXYWY2L

https://www.amazon.co.uk/dp/171793269X

HomiGenesis Signature

Covering the birth, nurturing and early growth of the unique

'Homigenesis - An Uniquely Individual Male Perspective' philosophy

Encompassing and developing the following key concepts;

Individual - Empathic - Gregarious - Thoughtful - Appreciative – Holistic

Presented & promoted via a combination of 1) academic research papers and specially created business, 2) Case studies, popular published **3)** e-books & 4) p-books, 5) formal lectures, 6) informative seminars, 7) Knowledge exchange presentations, 8) keynote speeches and 9) consultancy & 10) coaching.

Hashtags

#Homigenesis,

Ecclesiast - Hominist
Individuateur - Originateur - PrintMediateur – TechnoPreneur - Communicateur

Research Formats
Insights - Spotlights - Signposts - Pathways - Foresights - Scenarios – Opportunities

Jaeger (1,000)   Chronologs (2,000)   **Genesis (5,000)**
Essays (10,000)   Stories (20,000)   Novels & Theses (80,000)

Each containing a uniquely innovative 'Homigenesis Moment' for
Ecclesiast - Hominist - Individuateur - Originateur
PrintMediateur – TechnoPreneur - Communicateur

See also and keep in touch on

Ecclesiast
Acquiring & Developing Knowledge via Community - Culture -Creativity - EnterPrise.

Hominist
: Acquiring & Developing Knowledge via Masculinity - Man - Male - Manly -Manliness.

Individuateur
Acquiring & Developing Knowledge via Data - Information - Analysis - Knowledge.

Originateur
Acquiring & Developing Knowledge via Originality - Lifelong Learning -Transculturation – Innovation

PrintMediateur
Acquiring & Developing Knowledge via Channel - Media - Marketing - Print.

TechnoPreneur
Acquiring & Developing Knowledge via Capacity - Capability - Competence - Opportunity.

Communicateur
Acquiring & Developing Knowledge via

Thank you for reading

Billions will be Repaid to Millions – TimeOutCreditCards – Eric Leenders

"""It should be easier for consumers to challenge unfair agreements and that the definition of 'extortionate' should be widened to cover unfair practices both at the time of entering the credit agreement as well as any subsequent events that may have led to unfairness""".

Part of GlobalMeHPTE, Greater Eccles, Manchester, United Kingdom.

Homigenesis

Ecclesiast - Hominist - Individuateur - Originateur
PrintMediateur – TechnoPreneur - Communicateur

Tele: +44 7770 762860   Fax: + 44 161 789 8787

E-Mail: timeoutcreditcards@globalmehpte.com,

Words – 6,685   Images - 25   Pages – 41

Saturday 28th July 2018

TimeOutCreditCards Collateralised Credit Exploitation – The Financial Scandal of our Generation

Financial Slavery by Credit Card Companies

No financial organization has the right to make excessive interest & charges on nominal amounts that cannot be paid back within an individual's lifetime.

Find Out More On: https://bit.ly/2KWhfSu @TimeOutCCards @DisCreditCards *and/or*
TimeOutCreditCards: The Story So Far No. 1 https://www.amazon.co.uk/dp/B01N393PDI
What The FCA Should Know About Credit Cards https://www.amazon.co.uk/dp/B073Z1YVNT
Chronolog : Financial Slavery to Credit Cards https://www.amazon.co.uk/dp/B07FM664XV
Chronolog: 'Talk To Us, Prime Minister' https://www.amazon.co.uk/dp/B07FC2TJHY
Genesis: Billions will be REPAID to Millions – Amy Lenander – Capital One
https://www.amazon.co.uk/dp/171786273X

www.ingramcontent.com/pod-product-compliance
Lightning Source LLC
Chambersburg PA
CBHW040335220526
45473CB00009B/2686